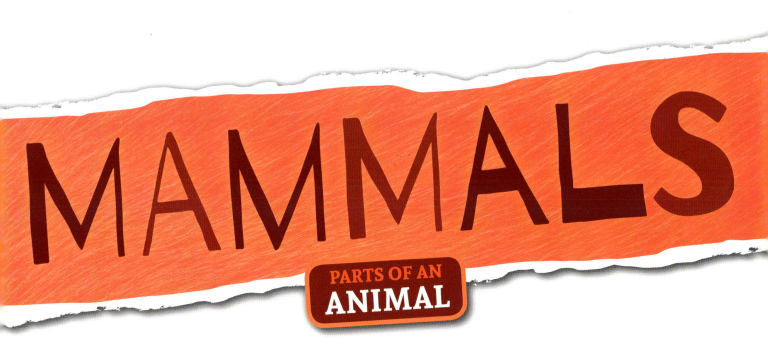

MAMMALS

**PARTS OF AN
ANIMAL**

Written by Emilie Dufresne

PHOTO CREDITS

Front Cover – Kit Korzun, Zhiltsov Alexandr, Redmich, Ondrej Chvatal, Dmitri Ma, Mikhail Kolesnikov, KatePh, 2 – Vaclav Sebek, 3 – J HIME, 4 – Dudarev Mikhail, 5 – Andrea Izzotti, Barbora Polivkova, Bernd Wolte, 6 – ArCaLu, 7 – vectorfusionart, Bobeh, BanayakoSensei, 8 – Jukka Jantunen, 9 – vkilikov, 10 – BlueRingMedia, 11 – Dwi Yoga Pujo Laksono, IanRedding, Melory, Tomas Palsovic, 12 – haveseen, 13 – philmillster, 14 – Ondrej Prosicky, 15 – Graeme Snow, 16 – Gelpi, 17 – Edward Young, 18 –Lisa Hagan, Breck P. Kent, 19 – Bildagentur Zoomar GmbH, 20 – Anna Veselova, 21 – Neil Bromhall, 22 – Syda Productions, 23 – iralu.

Images are courtesy of Shutterstock.com.
With thanks to Getty Images, Thinkstock Photo and iStockphoto.

BookLife
PUBLISHING

©2018
Book Life
King's Lynn
Norfolk PE30 4LS

ISBN: 978-1-78637-434-9

Written by:
Emilie Dufresne

Edited by:
Kirsty Holmes

Designed by:
Amy Li

A catalogue record for this book is available from the British Library.

All facts, statistics, web addresses and URLs in this book were verified as valid and accurate at time of writing. No responsibility for any changes to external websites or references can be accepted by either the author or publisher.

MAMMALS

Words that look like **this** can be found in the glossary on page 24.

WHAT IS A MAMMAL?

There are so many animals in the world that we split them into different **categories**. This helps us tell all of the animals apart.

One of these categories is mammals.

Groundhog

Bat

Dolphin

There are lots of different types of mammals.
They can live in the air, the sea, and even underground.

HOW DO YOU KNOW?

We can ask certain questions to find out if an animal is a mammal or not.

How do we know that

this is a mammal?

CHECKLIST

Does it have hair of some sort?

Does it give birth to live young?

Does it feed its babies with milk?

Is it warm-blooded?

IT'S A MAMMAL!

HEADS AND SHOULDERS

Humans are mammals, so we have similar faces and features to most mammals. Some have **adapted** these features to better suit where they live.

This moose has large **antlers** on its head made

from bone that are used to fight other moose.

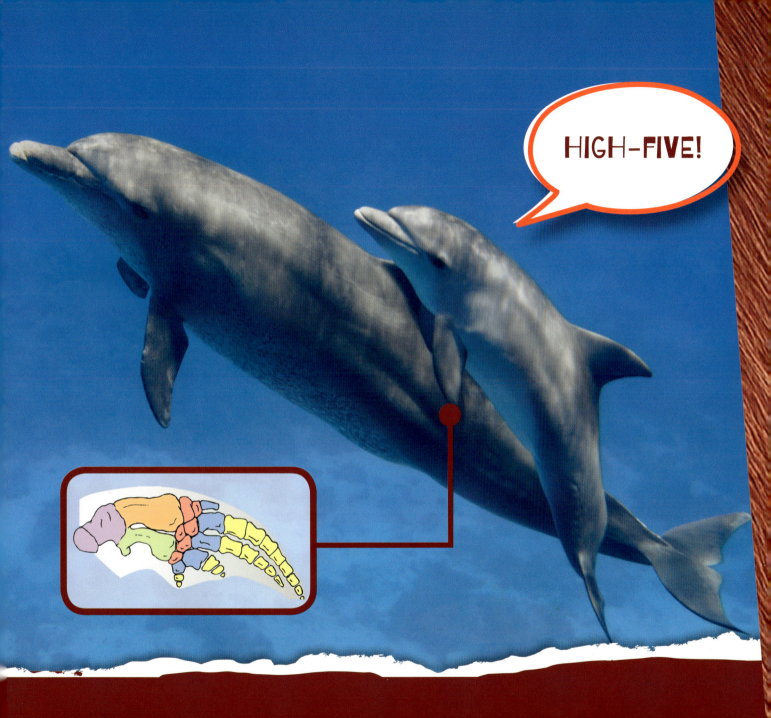

Even this dolphin's flipper has a shoulder joint and bones that **resemble** a human hand.

KNEES AND TOES

Lots of mammals are quadrupeds; they have four legs.
Their front legs have a shoulder, elbow and wrist.
Their back legs have a hip, knee and ankle, just like humans!

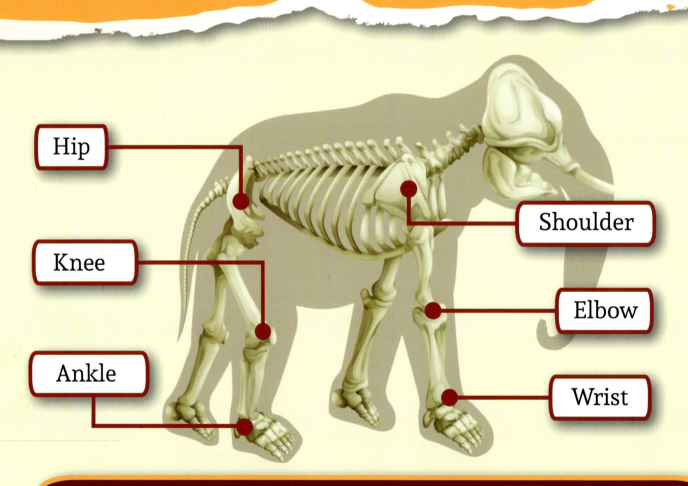

Hip

Knee

Ankle

Shoulder

Elbow

Wrist

The skeleton of this elephant is not that different from a human!

Hooves

Claws

Paws

Hands

Monkeys and humans have **opposable thumbs**!

Mammals have all different types of feet. Horses have hooves, bats have claws, bears have paws and monkeys have hands.

EYES AND EARS

Mammals usually have two eyes. This tarsier has big eyes that poke out from its head. They help it see better in the dark.

I THINK I'VE EATEN TOO MANY CARROTS...

Mammal ears have three parts; the outer ear, middle ear and inner ear. This cat's outer ear helps it hear extremely well. Mammals have fluid in their inner ear to help them balance.

MOUTH AND NOSE

Mammals' mouths are mostly used for breathing, eating and making sound. This anteater has a very long, thin tongue that can get into termite mounds.

29,999... 30,000! FINALLY FULL!

An anteater can eat up to 30,000 termites in a day!

Blow Hole

Blow holes are nostrils on top of their heads!

Most mammals have noses on the front of their heads and have a good sense of smell. Mammals that live in the sea don't have noses. They have blow holes!

SKIN

All mammals have some sort of hair on their body. For mammals that live on land, hair and fur helps to keep them warm and protect them.

We humans have hair on our heads to help

protect our skin from the Sun.

Honey badgers have hair all over their body that is thick and coarse. They also have very thick skin that helps protect them from predators.

MAMMALS THAT BREAK THE RULES

Marsupials are different to all other mammals. Marsupials give birth very early, and then let their young grow in a pouch.

Opossum

Baby Opossums

This opossum carries her babies in a pouch for up to 70 days.

Bill

PEOPLE USED TO THINK I WASN'T REAL; JUST LOTS OF ANIMALS STITCHED TOGETHER.

Platypuses are very strange mammals. They have a duck's bill, a beaver's tail and a body like an otter. They also lay eggs.

MIND-BOGGLING MAMMALS

This is an aye-aye. It is a **nocturna**l creature that finds its food by tapping on trees to find grubs.

For Tapping

For Digging

Its third finger is for tapping.

The fourth finger is for digging grubs out of trees.

Naked mole rats can live for up to 30 years.

They can live underground where there's not much oxygen.

They don't feel any pain on their skin.

This naked mole rat looks rather strange, but it has very interesting adaptations.

ACTIVITY

Think of some different animals. Use the checklist on page seven to see if they are mammals.

Remember that some mammals break the rules!

Has Outer Ears

Is Warm-Blooded

Has Fur

Once you find one that is a mammal, draw a picture of it.
Can you label what makes it a mammal?

GLOSSARY

ADAPTED	when something changes over time to suit its environment
ANTLERS	a pair of bony growths on the head of most deer
CATEGORIES	different sections within a larger group
NOCTURNAL	active at night instead of during the day
OPPOSABLE THUMBS	thumbs that can be moved around and touch the other fingers
RESEMBLE	to be similar to or look like

INDEX